a woman's place

Dear Bridget,

Thanks for everything.

Ling-Yen.

Auckland '93.

"I get the sense of her frustration of being a woman, of having limitations placed on her. She had tried to teach us (8 daughters) all the same thing: that girls must be independent, especially financially independent. She made sure we all got educated and held jobs."

"If they want to be heard… women must take the initiative and involve themselves actively in community work."

"We want to find out what is the Singapore woman's stand on family, career, our future, and try to develop a Singapore model which absorbs the best values of East and West."

"My husband prefers me to stay home. If he can afford, I also prefer to stay home and look after my baby. Home is more important. For my daughter, I want her to study. I also want her to marry, but must marry someone good."

"Women as a rule are not so prepared to make the sacrifices and commitment that political life demands. … [they] really have no reason to gripe as it is they themselves who shun the rough and tumble of the political arena."

"Women are still not accepted as equals. There hasn't been that fundamental change in attitude. So you can't take it easy. You have to keep trying to sensitise people [to the idea of equality]."

"Women and their families must be protected against unscrupulous husbands who treat their wives as chattels and abandon their children and families without any thought for their future."

for every woman's mother and father, son and daughter ...

A WOMAN'S PLACE
The Story of Singapore Women

A WOMAN'S PLACE
The Story of Singapore Women

© 1993 PAP Women's Wing

Published by
The PAP Women's Wing
510 Thomson Road #07-02 SLF Building
Singapore 1129

Editors
Aline Wong
Leong Wai Kum

The text is based on the research findings in the book *Singapore Women: Three Decades of Change* (1993, Times Academic Press), another project of the PAP Women's Wing.

The contributors of *Singapore Women* are:

Singapore Women: An Overview
Aline Wong and Leong Wai Kum
Marriage and Family
Stella Quah
Economic Participation
Linda Low, Toh Mun Heng, Euston Quah and David Lee
The Homemaker and the Economy
Euston Quah, David Lee, Linda Low and Toh Mun Heng
Older Women: From Colonial Times to Present Day
Ann Wee, assisted by Janet Yee
Demographic and Socio-Economic Characteristics of Older Women
G. Shantakumar
Legal Status
Liew Geok Heok and Leong Chooi Peng
Public Life and Leadership
Wang Look Fung and Nancy Teo, assisted by Lydia Goh

Project Coordination
Shova Loh

Text
Eng Wee Ling

Art Direction
Tuck Loong

Graphics
Loo Chuan Ming

Designed and produced by
Times Editions
Times Centre, 1 New Industrial Road, Singapore 1953

Distributed by
Shing Lee Publishers Pte Ltd
120 Hillview Avenue #05-06/07, Kewalram Hillview, Singapore 2366
Tel: 7601388 Fax: 7625684

Colour separation by Magenta Lithography
Printed in Singapore by Star Standard Industries Pte Ltd

ISBN 981 204 453 1

CONTENTS

Singapore is a young country but our development has been so rapid that we now face some issues which are similar to those in more advanced countries. Among these is how to further raise the status of women to become equal with the men. Women's status may be gauged from their legal status, educational opportunities, economic participation, political participation, roles in marriage, child rearing, homemaking and their security in old age.

This book tells the story of Singapore women and the struggles they have lived through. Women's issues are not isolated issues. They have profound implications for society and, indeed, for future generations. The book will also evoke some soul-searching. If women could live their lives all over again, would we still do it the way we did? Have we gained more than we have lost? What lessons can the young learn from us? There are no easy answers. But it is imperative that we pause from time to time to ask such questions, or we may lose touch and fail to grasp the momentous changes in our lives.

This is a record of the legacy built up by labours of love so that future generations may continue to thrive. Knowing the path traversed by our mothers and grand-mothers will help us make wiser choices for ourselves and our children. Building upon our parents' legacy is the next step forward.

MARRIAGE AND FAMILY
The Total Package

TYING THE KNOT

How or why the rites of marriage started is anybody's guess. An image that often springs to mind is that of a caveman clubbing a woman of his choice on her head, knocking her unconscious and dragging her off to his cave where they would live, maybe not so happily, ever after. We certainly hope such a barbaric practice never existed, but even if it did, it had already been outmoded a long time ago. Any man who tries that sort of thing today will quickly land himself in jail.

Marriage is more than a civil contract, it is a life-long commitment. Asian customs (overleaf) such as the sanctifying of marriage in a temple, the feasting of friends and relatives to share the family's joy, and the tea ceremony to honour older family members reflect the importance of this step.

These days, a marriage is a legally binding contract between two consenting adults who are at least 18 years old. The couple usually regard their marriage as their own private business. Not so in the old days. A marriage was to unite not just two people, but two families. Hence, the selection of a spouse was of great importance to the families and could not be left to chance and circumstance.

The reasons for marrying may vary from person to person and from one era to another, but most people still prefer being married to staying single. Marriage is a valued social institution.

What *has* changed over the years is that women are marrying later and there is an increasing proportion of single women between the ages of 30 and 34. Back in the 1950s, about 30 in every 100 girls between the ages of 15 and 19 were married, whereas in 1990, only about 1 in 100 were. Today, the average age of the groom is 28 years and that of the bride, 26 years. This is because most people regard economic security and emotional maturity as prerequisites for marriage, and a high level of education is necessary for women as well as men to succeed in life. In addition, with economic independence, marriage is viewed more as an option than a necessity.

Vasanthi, 35, mid-level civil servant: *"One of the best things Singapore has done for me is to give me an education because I'm independent and marriage is an option."*

It used to be that financial security was the main reason for women to marry. A common hope for daughters was that they would marry well. The other reason was to have children who would continue the family line and who were expected to take care of their parents eventually. Marriage and procreation were, basically, part of the survival process. The notions of love, courtship and romance were quite alien to Asian cultures.

Is this the right one? Young people wonder about relationships and love.

These days, most people marry for love and companionship. Men and women go to school or to work, allowing ample opportunity for them to meet and select their own spouses. There is hardly any need for the traditional forms of matchmaking where bride and groom could be strangers even on the wedding day. But not everyone is gregarious and some people work in jobs that are simply not conducive to meeting members of the opposite sex, hence the presence of the Social Development Unit and various private

agencies which try to determine compatibility as well as provide opportunities for men and women to meet. The popularity of these services attests to the fact that, given a choice and the right person, most people would like to be married.

Thus, many women are single not because they have anything against men or marriage, but because they never felt the need to marry, or they had not met a suitable man, or because they had missed opportunities.

Rosalind Heng, 48, principal of Singapore Chinese Girls' School: *"When my father died, as the eldest, I took over a lot of responsibilities. Over the years, during those susceptible moments, I was too caught up with too many things, so those moments passed."*

19

Siew Eng, 35, marketing manager: *"I'm a romantic. I need to be madly, deeply in love with a man in order to marry him. Most men I've met … there's no chemistry between us."*

Some women ask themselves whether they might have missed out on anything by not marrying, and if they might regret it when they grow old. Of course, when they see friends and family members who are happily married, they think they would like to be in their shoes, but when married friends divorce or when they have 'problem' children, they are relieved not to be laden with the same burden. In short, many of them do not have an answer.

Singapore women, on the whole, still have traditional family values, although how they balance these values with their personal goals and aspirations has led to later marriages and fewer children.

While the government may be justified in worrying about the growing group of 35-year-old singles, it should be noted that this is a worldwide phenomenon. Any official effort to persuade women to marry and have children should be sensitive to women's needs and aspirations. Above all, single women should never be made to feel they have less to contribute to society.

Is going solo through life desirable? is a question best answered by the individual. But where singlehood is because of a lack of opportunity, the Social Development Unit, begun in 1984, is a matchmaker extraordinaire – organising classes such as wine-drinking, outings flavoured with fun and exercise, and publishing *Link*, a quarterly magazine for its members, 13,000 in March 1993 and still growing.

The more you have
The more they need

Two is enough

Family Planning/Sterilisation Information Service

Campaigns for small families in the 1960s and 1970s (see posters at top and bottom) were replaced in the 1980s by exhortations to couples to have more children and to have them early (below and opposite). Early or late, parenthood is a special time.

MOTHERHOOD

Studies have shown that women value being a mother as much as being a wife. It is another indication that Singapore women still treasure family values.

But two things have changed in the last 30 years. One is the definition of the ideal family size; the other is the tendency for educated mothers to have small families.

The ideal family size may vary from person to person, and from community to community. Chinese, Malays and Indians in the old days, before the 'Stop At Two' campaign of the 1960s started, liked having large families. In 1970, the average number of children among all the ethnic groups was 4. This ideal number has dropped steadily over the years to fewer than 3 in 1990. In the mid-1980s, the government shifted its policy from encouraging smaller families to promoting the idea of larger ones.

It appears that the better-educated the woman, the fewer children she wants. This is true across the board, even among Malays who traditionally favour large families.

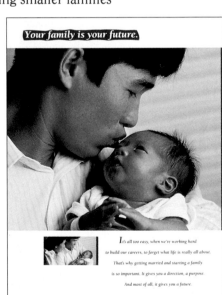

Your family is your future.

It's all too easy, when we're working hard
to build our careers, to forget what life is really all about.
That's why getting married and starting a family
is so important. It gives you a direction, a purpose.
And most of all, it gives you a future.

Educated women are most likely to be the ones who postpone marriage to pursue higher education or a career and they also tend to view motherhood in terms of quality rather than quantity. They want to be mothers but not to too many children. Unlike most of their mothers and grandmothers, they do not measure their personal fulfilment solely by their roles as wives and mothers. While many still would like their children to look after them in their old age, they no longer expect financial support from them.

「讓
我們之間
多隔幾年」

生女或生男
兩個就夠了

"I tell my children that I expect them to look after me, just as I look after their grandparents." —Laura Hwang, 40-something, former banker whose new career allows more time for the family

"I love children! But I don't expect my son to look after me in my old age. He'll have his own life to live." —Su Lan, 44

"I grew up thinking it's only natural to have children. My mother took very good care of my brother and me, so I want children to care for as well. When I grow older, they'll be companions to me. But I don't expect financial support from them." —Zainah, a 24-year-old doctor, recently married and with no children as yet

"I don't want children yet. I want to be able to spend time with my husband alone. Marriage is a very serious commitment, my life career, a permanent thing. I've stopped reading women's magazines that undermine marriage. There's nothing wrong with depending on each other for emotional support." —Patricia, 23, editor of a teen magazine, recently married

Young woman with child. Robert Burns called women 'Nature's noblest work'.

MARRIAGE AND WORK

Work is necessary for survival and women have always worked – be it in or outside the home.

There is some historical evidence that work used to be divided along gender lines, but both men's and women's work were considered to be equally important. Times change, however, and the nature of the work changed as well. Families no longer depended solely on their own ability to farm and hunt to survive. With industrialisation, men began to find jobs outside the home to earn money to support the family. As their jobs became more complex, men had to learn special skills.

Meanwhile, the nature of women's work on the home front did not change much. Their work, which was primarily housework and child care, did not earn them money and without money their work had less prestige than the men's. In the last few decades, though, women began to catch up with men. They, too, learnt new skills and found jobs outside the home.

The great quantity required of festival foods such as tarts and rice cakes for the Muslim celebration of Hari Raya Puasa calls for the hands of every family member, male and female. While yet another batch of tarts cools on trays, father and children make rice-cake casings out of coconut leaves, closely supervised by mother.

Opposite: Prayer for the whole family is often the woman's responsibility.

In the early years, it was the trend for women to work after completing their education but, once they were married, most of them stopped work to look after the home. Few returned to work. The traditional thinking that the home is the woman's responsibility is very strong and women see themselves having to play two roles, while men are only expected to be breadwinners and nothing more. In 1990, 0.2 percent (or 2 in a thousand) of all men compared to 32 per cent (or 320 in a thousand) of all women were full-time homemakers.

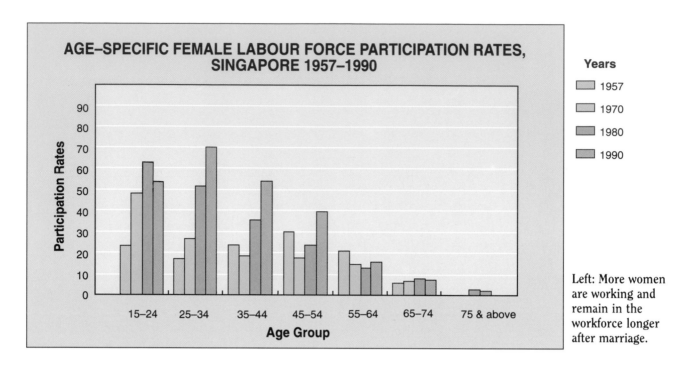

AGE–SPECIFIC FEMALE LABOUR FORCE PARTICIPATION RATES, SINGAPORE 1957–1990

Years
- 1957
- 1970
- 1980
- 1990

Left: More women are working and remain in the workforce longer after marriage.

But instead of letting these opposing interests rend their lives into different compartments, women, single and married, are increasingly determined to handle both home and job at the same time. The proportion of economically active single women doubled, from 25 percent in 1957 to 55 percent in 1990, while among married women the proportion more than tripled, from 14 percent to 43 percent.

Women work for a number of reasons. They treasure economic independence and the sense of achievement. They also work to supplement the family income and to be able to afford little luxuries for their loved ones.

Many divorced and widowed women who do not have a male breadwinner at home have to work mostly out of necessity. The proportion of economically active divorced women has jumped from 48 percent in 1970 to 67 percent in 1990. The figures for widows, however, have remained fairly constant at about 15–16 percent since 1970. This is probably because most women are widowed in their old age.

> Su Lan, now 44, married at 21 and was a full-time housewife for seven years before starting a small business, although her husband continued to be the main provider. Then when her husband died, she had to support herself and her two-year-old son. Three and a half years ago, she remarried, and although now she can afford not to work, she likes the independence that her job brings.

TILL DIVORCE DO US PART

Marriages have to be maintained by couples working hard at their partnership. Still, something may happen and they have to part.

There are more divorces these days in terms of absolute numbers, but as a percentage of the total female population, it is still a very small proportion – only 1.5 percent in 1990. Singapore has two sets of divorce laws, the Women's Charter for non-Muslims and Muslim Law, administered by the Syariah Court. The Muslim and non-Muslim divorce laws and proceedings are quite different.

For the last 30 years, the rate of divorce among Muslims has been higher than that for non-Muslims. Muslims also tend to divorce at a younger age. It may be that divorce and remarriage are more accepted among Muslims than among Chinese and Indians, but it is also because Muslim couples tend to marry at a younger age. When couples are still teenagers, they find it harder to take on the responsibilities of marital and parental roles.

A Muslim marriage that ends in divorce also tends to have lasted shorter than a non-Muslim marriage that ends in divorce. This may be because a Muslim couple does not have to wait the minimum period of three years before filing for divorce, unlike the requirement for non-Muslims under the Women's Charter.

An interesting fact is that there are more divorced women than men. This is a common phenomenon even in Western countries and it is because there is, in varying severity, prejudice against divorced women, which makes it much harder for them to remarry.

But why the increasing number of divorces? Those who are going through or who have gone through a divorce are usually reluctant to talk about their divorces as it is considered washing dirty linen in public. If at all possible, no matter what the real cause of the marriage breakdown, most prefer no-fault, uncontested divorces. Some people blame it on the fact that women are better-educated, and consequently demand equality in their marriage and are less tolerant of their husbands' misdeeds and marital injustices. The statistics, however, do not bear this out. As a matter of fact, the proportion of divorced persons with post-secondary education is extremely low.

FAMILY LIFE

Hearth and Home

Right after the war, the housing situation in Singapore was pretty dismal, especially in the city area. Homes were densely packed and there was little privacy. There were, on average, two families or 10 persons living in each house or flat.

There have been vast improvements in our housing conditions since Independence. With the growth of the economy and the expansion of the public housing programme, it is now the norm for each family to live in its own home. There are also much fewer people in each household. All this means greater comfort and more space.

The trend of nuclear families (husband, wife and their children) living on their own has been rising steadily over the years, from 64 percent of all households in 1957 to over 80 percent in 1990. Nowadays, the three-tier family – that is, grandparents, parents and grandchildren all living together – is far less common, accounting for only 14 percent of all households. The thought of living in a very large household does not appeal to most young people as they wish to retain their privacy and run their own lives.

Divorced and widowed persons are much more likely to live in three-tier families than those who are single or married. One reason could be a need for the emotional and financial support that an extended family brings. Divorcees with young children will no doubt be grateful to have someone help with the childcare while they go out to work.

Opposite: Eight out of ten of us belong to nuclear families living in HDB flats. The days of large extended families living in kampungs (below left) are past.

Overleaf: Father minds the baby while mother coaches baby's big sister. Such sharing of family chores makes the woman's decision to continue working outside the home easier.

Rocking the Cradle

Most people believe that, ideally, parents should be the ones to take care of their children. However, the ideal is not always achievable, given the reality of working mothers. Hence parents may have to resort

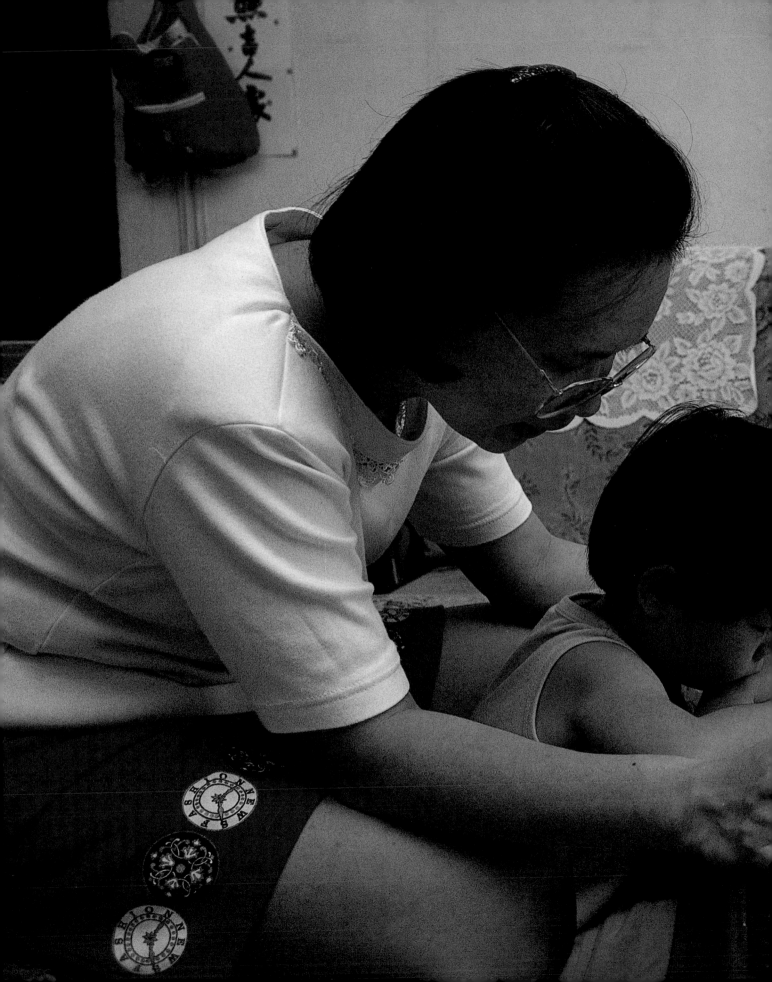

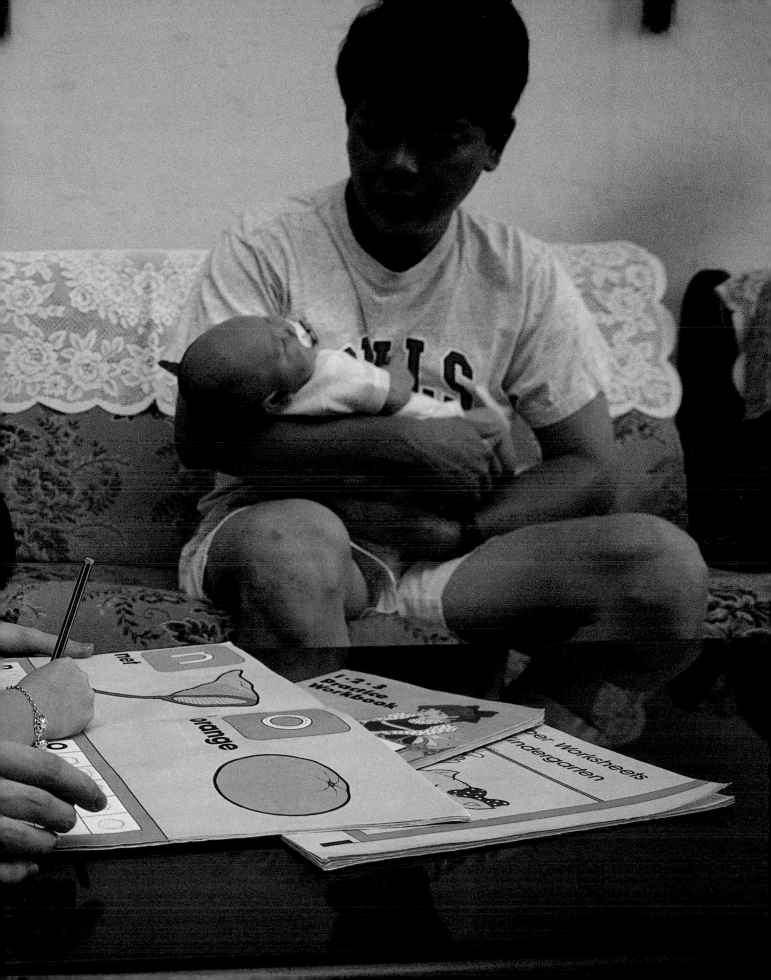

to alternative childcare arrangements. Their preferences are to turn to grandparents first, then maids, foster mothers, childcare centres and, as a last resort, they may have to leave their children on their own. Of the three main ethnic groups, Malay parents are the most inclined to look after their children themselves.

The childcare arrangement adopted by parents also varies according to the age of the child. The trend is for babies below the age of one to be cared for by the parents. Thereafter, help is enlisted from grandparents or relatives, until about the time when the child turns 7. By then, children would require less supervision and parents would again care for them on their own.

"My mother worked when we were growing up and we were looked after by an 'adopted' grandmother. After that she looked after us herself. I don't believe in letting a maid bring children up, although I intend to work, like my mother did. I'm sure my parents and in-laws will help." —Zainah

Working women who marry and have children feel they have to play many roles and excel in each and every one of them. Clearly this requires women to be superwomen, which is not possible. Sooner or later, something will give way.

Therefore, if we want women to continue working and have more children as well, the society must help the family to cope. Since parents prefer to look after their children themselves and this is highly recommended by psychologists, mothers and fathers should be encouraged to share the responsibility of childcare. There should be greater flexibility in working hours and job contracts to allow them to discharge this responsibility. More childcare centres would be of help too.

When it comes to babysitting, relatives are a boon (left). An increasing number of families hire foreign maids (seen above congregating in their favourite day-off spot at Orchard Road) or send their toddlers to day-care centres (opposite).

Time to Relax

Leisure time is free time and it usually means time outside work. But what is or is not work is sometimes not so easily distinguished.

It is easy enough for men. More often than not, the moment they leave their work places they are 'free'. It is different for women. For a full-time homemaker, her home is her work place, so there's no 'leaving work' as such. Moreover, the nature of housework and child-care, especially while the children are young, takes up all her waking hours. A woman who holds a job outside the home still has to spend her non-working hours on housework, so in effect, her 'off-work' hours are working hours as well. Women's work is, truly, never completely done.

It is comforting that Singapore women, for all their modernity, still retain their family values. The home and family continue to be of great importance to them. At the same time, they want to work, to achieve and improve themselves. But the multiple roles that women are expected to play are a tremendous burden.

Women all over the world are learning that they cannot do it all by themselves. Perhaps the time is also ripe for others to realise this too. Don't think of it as just helping the women; think of it as helping everyone around them as well, because a fulfilled person is a better person and a fulfilled woman will be a better wife and a better mother. And the hand that rocks the cradle rules the world.

Leisure means quiet time for some (preceding pages), family walks and rides (opposite), or get-togethers of the clan on birthdays (above) or just for fun (right).

EDUCATION AND EMPLOYMENT
Keys to Success

Education opens the window of opportunity. Adults at Li Mei's (opposite) BEST – Basic Education for Skills Training – class are aware of this and try to make up for their lost years. Better late than never.

But better early than late. Parents these days make sure their daughters (below and right) get the best education they can afford.

EDUCATING DAUGHTERS

In the old days, very few women received an education.

"Girls, when they get married, they're other people's property. So no need to waste money educating them. You'll benefit the man's side." —Mrs Loh, 81 years old

If girls did receive an education, it was either because the family was unusually well-to-do or unusually enlightened. One such example is Mrs Puthucheary, 78, a Singaporean Indian raised in a wealthy family, who had private tutors at home. Some families, like hers, believed in educating their daughters, but it was generally to increase their value as brides and not to equip the girls for gainful employment. Young women in those days could not even step out of the house to go to the market unaccompanied, much less go to work.

In the early days of Singapore, the attitude towards education for women was generally one of indifference. It wasn't until the later part of the 19th century that things began to change. Various Christian missions set up schools here and the first all-girl government school, Raffles Girls' School, was founded. But the very first all-girl school to be set up by private individuals was the Singapore Chinese Girls' School founded in 1899. It came about because a group of Peranakan (Straits Chinese) businessmen saw the need to educate their

daughters. At that time, girls were still seen to be, economically speaking, unproductive and it would therefore be a waste of money to educate them.

"But these businessmen were enlightened and wanted for their daughters at least a primary [school] education and be able to read, write, speak Chinese and Malay, sew, cook and generally be 'Kim Geks'," recounts the present principal of the school, Miss Rosalind Heng.

39

In Hokkien, *kim* means gold and *gek* means jade. For the Peranakans, a girl who was a 'Kim Gek' would be the very embodiment of the traditional Chinese virtues of filial piety, gentility, kindness, propriety and diligence. In short, she would make a good wife, mother and daughter-in-law.

The idea that education should encompass more than feminine virtues, however, was uppermost with the founder of the Nanyang Girls' High School. Mr Chen Chunan was inspired by Chinese revolutionary Dr Sun Yat Sen's comments on the lack of women's involvement in the movement to establish the Republic of China, owing to their lack of education. The school began in 1917 with only about 100 students. In time, the enrolment grew. By 1931, the school introduced secondary education for their girls. As early as the 1930s, girls educated in Chinese schools such as this were already encouraged to participate in sports and oratorical competitions, a new strategy to nurture leadership qualities.

Nevertheless, before World War II, school enrolment for girls was never too stable because the parents' main aim was to train their girls to be good housewives. A Primary 6 education was generally considered sufficient.

Mrs Seow Peck Leng, born 1911: *"My cousins never had any education, so I was considered the 'naughty girl'! I was in Raffles College, one of the four or five women among 400 men. So naturally my friends were mainly men. My auntie did not approve of my education. When I was studying, I used to get a scolding from my auntie. She would say, 'You read your books and no one will want to marry you. When your mother-in-law asks you to cook rice, you show her the book and tell her you're studying.'"*

Reflecting the changing face of education from turning out *kim geks* to women of substance, intellect and style is the metamorphosis of the SCGS school uniform from little kebayas (1913 picture above) to samfoos (1948, right), to the modern-day sundress (1990, left).

After the war, in response to the social and political changes and new economic demands, girls' schools began to have proper Senior Cambridge (equivalent to the present-day 'O' level) classes. The syllabus emphasised the three R's – reading, 'riting and 'rithmetic – and the sciences were introduced.

In SCGS, the uniform changed from little kebayas to a blue and white samfoo and, as if to herald the new era, to the present

light blue sundress. Miss Heng, who was born after the war, 48 years ago, is a product of the new era. Being the eldest in the family, there was never any doubt in her father's mind that she would be a university graduate. After her father's death when she was just 18, her mother further drummed it into her that it was her responsibility to enter the university and set a good example for her younger siblings.

EQUAL PAY FOR EQUAL WORK

By then, education was no longer just to produce good wives, but a means to an independent livelihood as well. Unfortunately, in most instances, working women were getting a raw deal in terms of pay and status. For example, women in both the private and government sectors got a mere fraction of what the men received for similar work. And women in the civil service such as teachers, regardless of seniority, would be reduced to 'temporary' status upon marriage and have their pay reduced accordingly.

As the number of women going to work began to grow, inevitably, so did discontent with the treatment of employed women. Some women began to speak out against the discrimination. In 1959, during the election to the Legislative Assembly, the People's Action Party promised, as one of their platforms, to work towards equal pay for women who did equal work as men.

These days, women expect nothing less than equal pay for equal work, but back in 1959, this was a revolutionary concept. Not everyone was prepared to have women working alongside men, much less draw the same wages.

In response to Mrs Lee Kuan Yew's radio broadcast that the PAP supported the principle of equal pay for equal work, a letter to the press read, *"The only conclusion that one can draw from the extraordinary speech by Mrs Lee Kuan Yew is that she has a very vivid imagination. If she thinks that a woman's place is not in the home, then where is it? In the office and in the field? … Does the PAP intend to look after our children for us while we toil side by side with the men wearing the same type of clothes?"* —'ABC' in *The Malay Mail*, 13 May 1959

On 15 November 1961, the newspapers reported that the PAP Women's Affairs Bureau had submitted a four-page memorandum to the Minister for Finance, urging equal treatment for women in the civil service. Among other things, they asked that men and women be on the same pay scale, that marriage

Today, either studying in the library at the National University of Singapore (above) or in discussion with other students in a tutorial at the Singapore Polytechnic (below), women students at institutions of higher learning are a common sight.

should not affect a woman's status in the civil service, and that the age of retirement be the same for men and women.

In 1962, in recognition of the fact that women do work as hard as men, as well as to encourage more women to enter the workforce, the government announced that it was going to implement a policy of equal pay for equal work in the civil service. Naturally, there was much doubt and apprehension as to whether such a bold move would actually work. There was also a deep-seated prejudice against working women. These doubts proved to be unfounded and by the 1970s, some men found themselves working as subordinates of women.

HIGHER EDUCATION FOR WOMEN

The most important factor that contributed to the success of women was the government's policy of universal education, for boys and girls alike. By the mid-1960s, Singapore's education policies were well established. New schools were quickly built to accommodate the growing number of children, school

43

fees were, and still are, heavily subsidised to make education affordable to all, and the University of Singapore was expanding to create new faculties for disciplines not previously offered. The opportunities for all, male and female, were there and the criterion for entry into institutions of higher learning was based on merit.

From one-quarter to about half the total enrolment at institutions of higher learning (below left), the growing presence of women means they can be found in practically every course or discipline offered. While there are still male-dominated disciplines such as Engineering and Medicine, it is becoming increasingly common to find women in these and other related disciplines such as Biotechnology (top left).

The proportion of girls to boys enrolled at all educational levels has risen considerably over the last three decades. The change is dramatic. In 1991, there were as many girls as there were boys enrolled in secondary schools. At the tertiary level, there were only 34 women to 100 men in 1960. By 1991, this had risen to 73:100. Today, women outnumber men in some subjects like Arts and Social Sciences and Accountancy. In Accountancy, there are three times as many women as there are men. There are, however, still the traditionally male disciplines such as Medicine and Engineering, where the men outnumber the women 2 to 1 and 5 to 1 respectively.

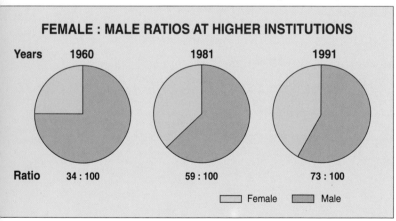

FEMALE : MALE RATIOS AT HIGHER INSTITUTIONS

Years	1960	1981	1991
Ratio	34 : 100	59 : 100	73 : 100

Female   Male

These days, families expect their daughters, the way they have always expected their sons, to study hard and, if they can, to enter the university. This 180-degree turn is remarkable by any standards, and the fact that it happened in just three decades is truly incredible.

What made Singaporeans place such a high priority on the education of their sons and daughters? The answer is a combination of a whole host of factors. Singapore has no other resource but its people. This was felt even more acutely after the country gained independence in 1965. We have no land to mine for ore and no crops to harvest for export. The government knew that industrialisation would have to be the key to our survival and Singaporeans would have to be educated and skilled if the economy were to develop.

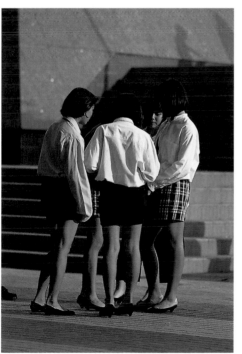

Everyone had to pitch in. So women became educated and they went to work. And they liked the independence and feeling of pride that the ability to earn money brought. Women were spending their own and not their husbands' money; they were contributing financially to their family. All that gave them more control over their lives. Women began to enjoy a higher status at home and in society and with higher status came greater willingness on the parents' part to educate them.

Women realised that education and employment based on meritocracy meant that the opportunities were there for their picking if they were good enough and if they tried hard enough. Parents, too, began to have aspirations for their daughters. Educated daughters could earn as much as sons and, like sons, they could become independent as well as contribute to the family.

Parents also discovered that in a compact island like Singapore, daughters who are 'married out' are never very far away. They do come back after all and they do not become 'other people's property'. Even Mrs Loh, who said educating daughters was a waste of money, feels proud when her granddaughters excel in their studies.

THE RIGHT TO ACHIEVE

As a reflection of the rapidly changing times, expectations of women have changed as well. Schools are not content merely to turn out good wives. As Miss Heng put it, they want to see their girls as 'women with substance, form, style and confidence'. They would also like them to be decent, honourable, magnanimous and compassionate. A tall order indeed and a long way from what education for girls used to mean.

We have certainly progressed a lot, yet somewhere along the way, some did miss out on the opportunities. In some pockets of society, parents had remained fairly oblivious to the changing times and needs. As a result, their children now feel that they have been deprived. But they were not discouraged.

With a host of options and opportunities before them, young women never had it so good. The education system is based on merit. If you have good grades, diligence and the desire, you can go as far as you are able, regardless of race, religion or gender.

Irene Goh, now 38, is the second child but eldest of five daughters in a family of seven children, who was taken out of school in Secondary 2. She tells her story with no bitterness, just a deep sense of loss and regret.

"My grandmother was old at that time and she wanted me to stop school to look after her. She said, 'Girl no need to study so much.' Since I didn't pass my Sec 2, my father also said I should stop to help look after my younger sisters and brother. So for nearly 10 years I stayed home, helped out with the housework, cooked and cleaned, did the washing and looked after my grandmother."

In about 1977, Irene took on her first paying job; it was with an electronics company. At the same time, she signed up for night classes at the Adult Education Board. It was tough, working in the day and studying at night, but she was determined. As she explains, *"I wanted to study because I felt that without education, it was very hard to find jobs."* So she took her Secondary 2 examinations again, passed that, and went on to complete her 'O' levels.

Irene married in 1981. She now has two children, a daughter aged 10 and a son aged 4. *"I want my daughter to study because it is necessary to have a good education before you can do anything. I will encourage her to go as far as she can. Maybe even go to the U. Education is equally important for boys and girls. I feel that all those years I spent at home have all been wasted. If I could live my life all over again, I wish I could go back to school, complete my education."*

These days, parents who do not educate their daughters are virtually non-existent. Try telling Yvonne Gomez, 16, or her sister Jessica, 18, that women do not need an education and you will draw blank, uncomprehending looks from them. To them, education is no longer a luxury, nor is it an option. It is a right.

But it is a right that has to be earned through hard work and discipline. Most young women understand how important education is. It is not something they take lightly, nor is it something they should forego just because they are women. They can see for themselves, and their parents remind them constantly, that education is the key to success in life.

Meg, a woman lawyer in her early 40s, takes great pride in the fact that she is a self-made woman. She did not go to the university after school as the family was rather low on funds at the time and her mother was not inclined to spend money on a daughter's education. But Meg had dreams and she had tenacity. She took the long, hard road by working as an articled clerk for six years in a law firm. In addition to this extended apprenticeship, she had to attend university lectures and tutorials for selected subjects to earn all her stripes.

Meg has good reason to be proud of herself and she takes great pleasure in reminding her mother that she would not be drawing the kind of salary that she does now, if not for her perseverance.

In sharp contrast is Zainah's mother, who encouraged and even tutored Zainah and her brother in Mathematics.

"My mother stopped at Sec 4. She wanted to further her education very badly but her family didn't have much money and they weren't keen for her to continue either. They told her if she had the money she could go on, but since she didn't, she had to work. That's why she's all out for our education."—Zainah

Traditionally, good jobs for women meant dispensing knowledge as teachers (left) or nursing the sick. These days, you find them in factories, offices and restaurants.

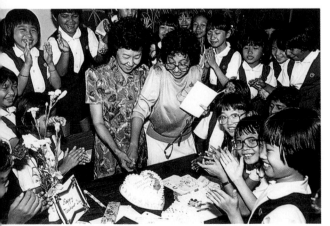

CHANGING WORK

The new attitude of parents and the widening education opportunities for women gradually and irrevocably changed the face of the national workforce.

The presence of women in the workforce has grown steadily over the years. In 1957, only 22 percent of all women above the age of 15 were economically active. By 1970, the figure rose to

Be it waiting for an 'air-con' bus to take her to an 'air-con' office or tackling greasy engines and flat tyres (opposite), more women are finding work.

Bottom right: We have more women working than in most other East and Southeast Asian countries.

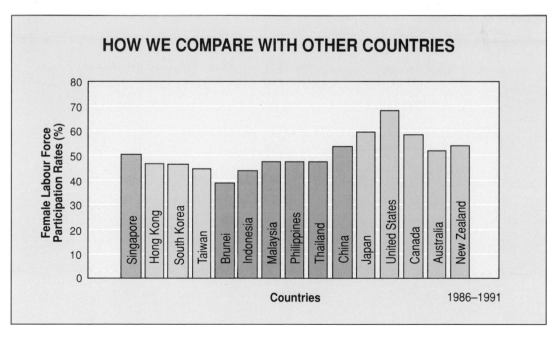

HOW WE COMPARE WITH OTHER COUNTRIES

Female Labour Force Participation Rates (%)

Countries   1986–1991

51

30 percent and by 1990, it leapt to 50 percent, which is higher than all the other ASEAN countries and even Hong Kong. Our proportion is closer to countries like Australia and New Zealand.

In the 1960s, women were primarily employed in lower-paying service jobs or repetitive ones like work on an assembly line and what were considered 'women's occupations' such as teaching, nursing and clerical work. In the 1970s, the percentage of women in the commercial and financial sectors improved a little, but the bulk of them were still in

manufacturing. The 1980s began to see more women in commerce and financial services so that while one-third of women are still in manufacturing, another third are now in business and finance.

Like the widening ripples of a pebble thrown into still water, the effects of the new education opportunities have now reached the rarefied zone of top administrative and managerial posts. Women may still be grossly under-represented in this traditional domain of men but, even here, they are making their presence felt.

Work on assembly lines is still predominantly performed by women (left), but the tables below and overleaf indicate the employment trend is towards more even participation by women in the various sectors.

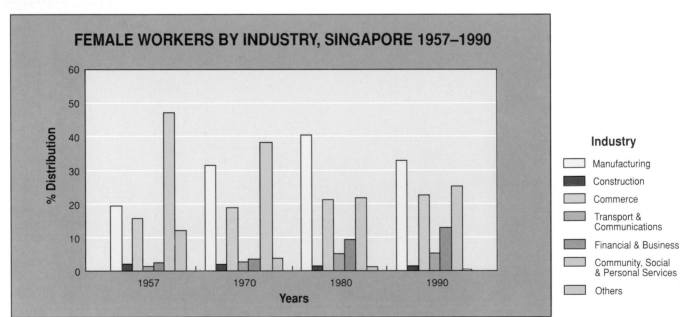

FEMALE WORKERS BY INDUSTRY, SINGAPORE 1957–1990

Industry

- Manufacturing
- Construction
- Commerce
- Transport & Communications
- Financial & Business
- Community, Social & Personal Services
- Others

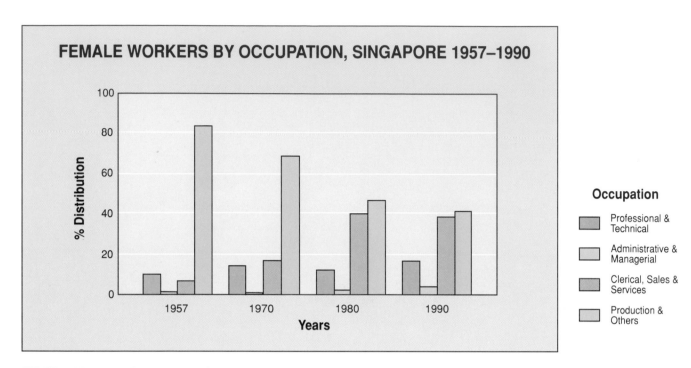

FEMALE WORKERS BY OCCUPATION, SINGAPORE 1957–1990

% Distribution (y-axis, 0–100)

Years (x-axis): 1957, 1970, 1980, 1990

Occupation
- Professional & Technical
- Administrative & Managerial
- Clerical, Sales & Services
- Production & Others

THE WAY TO THE TOP

It seems that, nowadays, few women actually experience any blatant gender discrimination in terms of education, recruitment, pay or advancement.

The wage gap between men and women has steadily decreased over the years although there is still a gap of about 30 percent in earnings. This gap will narrow further as more women acquire higher education, skills and seniority. All this takes time. The future looks rosy for the younger, educated woman poised to enter the workforce.

But the question remains: why are there still so few women at the top? True, there is little overt discrimination. It may be that a 'glass ceiling' exists because of men's attitudes towards women, which in some cases affect their chances for the further training and job enlargement that lead to promotion. Moreover, working women of today were brought up by mothers who themselves may have felt inferior to

In Singapore, as elsewhere, women make up the majority of the nursing strength in the hospitals, but they are making their presence felt as doctors, too. At right are a nurse and a consultant cardiologist, with a patient.

Bottom left: Women are still the main strength of our factory workforce.

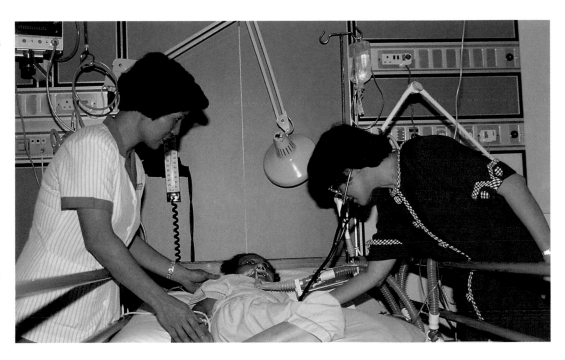

men and unintentionally passed on a sense of inferiority to them.

Traditionally, Asian women do not lead. They tend to follow. They also tend to keep silent when men talk; where there is a difference in opinion, they defer to the men. Moreover, women in most cultures are not expected to compete. The good news is, that is changing now. Women are learning to take charge. We have women role models in practically every area: in politics, in top executive levels, in the professions, and even on the High Court bench.

M'lord Is A Lady!

For someone who made history in Singapore by being the first woman to be appointed to the High Court bench, Ms Lai Siu Chiu is pleasantly modest and surprisingly matter-of-fact about it.

"I came out to practice in the early 1970s," she recounts. *"There were few women litigators then. In those days, perhaps, the thinking was that women lawyers should stick to the office and do conveyancing mainly. For me, maybe I didn't have the temperament to do conveyancing and, over the years, I just never got out of litigation. In 1977, I did my Masters in Shipping Law. In those days, there were no women shipping lawyers, and that in itself was a challenge to me."*

Like many other women, she faced the problem of juggling career and family responsibilities after her marriage and the birth of her children. *"I couldn't work at the same pace. I depended on domestic help."*

The one thing that truly impresses about Ms Lai is her commitment to her clients. When she was on maternity leave after delivering her second child, she had files sent to her home so that she could work on them. She believes that she must always be there for the clients. She only thought of quitting practice once, and even then, the thought terrified her because *"I was very involved in practice and I didn't know what I would do with myself."*

Although she is zealously committed to her profession, she is also thoroughly involved in the care of her children, one aged 8 and the other 4. She seems to have struck some kind of balance. *"It's not how much time I spend with them, but what I do with them. I sometimes wish there're more than 24 hours in a day but that's not possible so you do the best you can. Is it satisfactory? Well, it's the best balance in the circumstances."*

Her appointment at the age of 40-something is considered young, but she asks rhetorically, *"Has age anything to do with it?"* Or gender for that matter. The really relevant factors are experience and ability and she has shown during her 20 years of practice that she is a very skilled lawyer.

At present, Singapore has two women on the High Court: Ms Lai Siu Chiu and Mrs Judith Prakash. Three women ambassadors who have represented Singapore are Professor Chan Heng Chee, Mrs Jaya Mohideen, and Mrs Mary Seet-Cheng. They join the small number of women who are at the very top of their fields. The top rungs of general managers, chief executive officers, architects, engineers and some other professionals are still predominantly occupied by men but, given time, no doubt more women will work their way up there, too. Then, their growing number will be too big to ignore.

Ms Lai Siu Chiu (left) and Mrs Judith Prakash (right) are Singapore's first and second women Judicial Commissioners respectively.

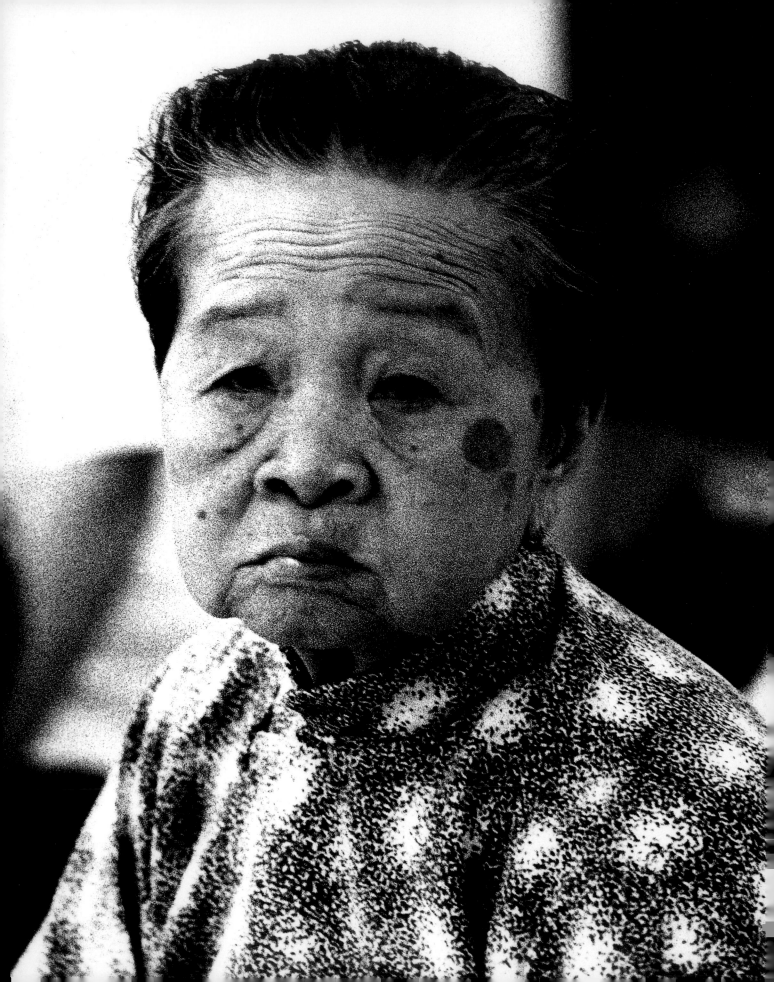

OLDER WOMEN
Planning for the Golden Years

Waiting for future to happen,
Waiting for past to end,
Waiting for husbands, fathers,
Children, friends.

Waiting, while life walks by,
Waiting, while death stays late,
Waiting, for everyone
We wait.

Waiting for nights to flee,
Waiting for days to call,
Waiting while oceans dry,
Waiting while mountains fall.

Waiting, for blood to wake,
Waiting, till eyes can see,
Waiting, eternally waiting
To be free.

—'Woman's Song: Doing Time' by Lee Tzu Pheng, from her collection, *The Brink Of An Amen*.

HER STORY

Sixty. The big SIX-O is generally considered the onset of old age. In Asian cultures older people are usually seen as wise, knowledgeable and dignified, and are therefore accorded much respect. In the days when birth control was non-existent, middle-aged women past reproductive age were also relieved of childbearing and childcaring responsibilities. Longevity is a blessing and it is a custom to celebrate the 60th birthday in a big way.

Even back in China, the life of the older Chinese woman was much better than that of the younger woman. As a young bride, she might be ill-treated and in any case had no status in the household. By the time she was old, however, she would have had sons, and daughters-in-law who would in turn attend to her. She would be entitled to respect and filial care. Although she could not ever own property, she was much revered and sometimes feared.

But 19th century life in Singapore being hard and short, it is unlikely the indigenous people – the Malays and boat-dwellers – lived to old age.

Later on, the Chinese and the Indians came, but they had no intention of making Singapore their home. They were here to make their fortunes and then return to their families in the homeland. So it was unlikely that they brought their aged with them or that they stayed on here in their own old age.

The 1871 census showed that, within a population of 97,000, there were only 559 older women: 360 Malay, 177 Chinese and 22 South Indians. Except for the Malays, none of the

History is everywhere: in the Hajjah Fatimah Mosque (right) – a silent testimony to what one woman can do with the right mix of piety and enterprise, in the wiry Samsui woman (below), and in the woman opposite, patiently stiching patch-work.

other older women were likely to have been Singapore-born.

The middle-aged women who had come to Singapore had a lot of freedom compared to those in the old country. Historians recorded that women went marketing and they rode on public transportation. They were also recorded as having been employed, among other things, as dressmakers, live-in amahs, fisherwomen and even 'planters, managers, overseers'.

Singapore's first identified woman of substance was Hajjah Fatimah, who is remembered to this day as the builder of the Hajjah Fatimah Mosque at Beach Road. After robbers burned down her house twice, she decided to erect a mosque on the site instead, employing a British architect and a French contractor. She carried on a trade and owned vessels, and built houses for her family and the poor. She lived to be 98.

The large population of single men who came to work without their families made prostitution a much documented female profession. Thankfully, there was also demand for other services that the women could provide. Women with sewing skills made a living patching trousers and jackets, while others provided laundry services, and so on.

In time, as some of the migrants stayed on and set up home in Singapore, the number of marriages and local weddings increased. In those days, most marriages were arranged and that made the matchmaker a very important person. Usually an older woman whose judgment of character would be respected, her knowledge of customs and traditions and her extensive social network made her services both essential and profitable.

Other older women with knowledge of traditional remedies sometimes served as 'consultants' on the use of herbs and such. Yet others served as spirit mediums and some became fairly wealthy from all the 'red packets' they received for their services.

There were also other women who defied the convention of the time and chose to stay single and independent. There were the Samsui women, petite and fragile-looking, but strong enough to be labourers in building construction. There were also the 'black-and-white'

Cantonese amahs, who are reputed to be unparalleled in their childminding and housekeeping skills. These women worked hard and were regarded to be almost as good as the men, not just in the way they worked, but also in their ability to save and send money home.

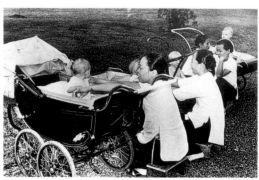

Working women in those days might have worked in humble jobs that younger workers today shun, but they remained fiercely independent and took great pride in the fact that, not only did they support themselves, they even supported their families back in their homeland.

NEW WORLD

In an age when they were expected to be subservient and dependent, these women – the 'black-and-white' amahs and the cabaret artiste – asserted their independence. So, too, working women like the one opposite and the karanguni woman (left).

In the decades following World War II, major changes occurred in the political and social arenas of many countries. The old ways were slowly being phased out and, like it or not, Singapore was caught up in the wave.

The Women's Charter was passed in 1961 and subsequent policies on universal education, female employment and family planning have improved the lives of women in Singapore dramatically. Since all these changes took place only within the last 30 years, those who have benefited most are younger women. But what about the older women who have not benefited directly from these policies? What can be done for them?

The proportion of aged women has increased from 6 percent to around 10 percent over the last two decades. This is due to the declining birthrate and a longer life expectancy. There are also more women in the 'extreme old age' group. Since women generally live longer than men, there are many widows in this group.

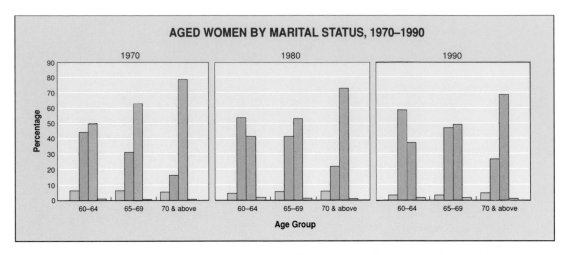

AGED WOMEN BY MARITAL STATUS, 1970–1990

This group is a cause for concern because it consists of women who had little or no education when they were young, few marketable skills, and no economic security. Being married improved their economic and social support. But since they tend to outlive their husbands, eventually they have to depend on their children. This is contingent upon the children being filial, of course.

OF HOME AND HEART

A basic life necessity is having a roof over one's head. This is even more critical in old age.

Home ownership has increased overall in Singapore due to the expansion of the public housing programme and financial schemes to help Singaporeans own homes. Similarly, the figures for home ownership have improved for all aged women, although single aged women, who form 3.5 percent of the population, have the lowest ownership rates at 60 percent, compared to 90 percent of married aged women. Despite housing schemes to cater to this group of elderly people, they are likely to have the least financial and social support. Society, therefore, has a responsibility to look more closely at their needs.

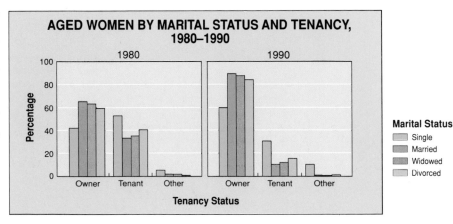

AGED WOMEN BY MARITAL STATUS AND TENANCY, 1980–1990

Since women tend to outlive men, there is a high percentage of widows aged 70 and over (left). Although most of them own homes (below left), there are still some women who have neither family nor financial security. Volunteer groups provide residential and day-care shelters such as the ones at right and below, but as pleasant as these may be, there is no substitute for the warmth of the family.

Poverty can strike aged widows too. Because most of them have been dependants, they have little or no income, no Central Provident Fund of their own, and may not even own their home.

In Singapore, the main financial security for old age is contributions to the CPF. Since the average aged woman of today either did not work for wages, or worked in low-paying jobs, she is unlikely to have saved very much. She will continue to be financially dependent on her spouse (if she is married) or her children, if they are filial and financially able. As she gets older and her health begins to fail, rising medical costs make the future look a little daunting, even though her children can help through their Medisave.

As important as economic support for the aged is social and emotional support. Fortunately, in Singapore, family support for the aged is still strong, and most aged women live with their children or relatives. In 1990, less than 4 percent of all aged women lived alone.

In contrast, 90 percent lived in multi-generation households. Their other children, who lived on their own, visited them regularly and provided financial support. Kinship ties remain very strong. The figures are heartening and should encourage greater efforts towards maintaining a strong family support network, especially in the face of our graying population.

NEVER TOO OLD TO EARN

In 1990, about 8 percent of women over 60 worked and earned wages. The better-educated women had higher incomes but average incomes fall across the board, the older one gets.

It is interesting that in the 1950s, older women tended to stay employed whereas now fewer of them work. This is partly due to the increasing need of the economy for better-educated and better-skilled workers who tend to be younger, and partly because of the decline of 'kampung' industries and small family enterprises drawing on family labour.

In the next decade, women who are now in their fifties will join the ranks of the old and their status could be an indication of what the future holds for the aged women. The younger women of today are much better-educated compared with their mothers and grandmothers. When they eventually become the older and aged women of the future, their education will stand them in good stead.

It is true for men as well as for women that the higher the education level, the better the chances of employment continuing into their old age. Moreover, the better-educated older women can be found in the better-paying professional and technical, administrative and managerial jobs. In these jobs, work performance need not be affected and, indeed, may be enhanced by age and experience, unlike clerical and production occupations.

SIXTY AND *SENANG*

Generally speaking, older people have more leisure time. If they are not working, and the children (if they have any) are grown up and independent, what do they do with all that free time?

Men and women seem to adjust differently to old age and retirement. It is quite common for men who have worked all their adult lives to find themselves suddenly at a loss when they cease employment. The absence of a job to go to every day and the reduction of income may cause them to feel unproductive and unimportant. Women, on the other hand, seem to have fewer adjustment problems. First of all, old age is not greeted with as much dread in our Asian cultures as it is in the West and the appearance of a few wrinkles is not a major catastrophe. Second, whether they worked in jobs outside the home or not, most women would have been responsible for the home and family members. Housework, caring for husband, children, grandchildren and so on are responsibilities for which there is no retirement age.

So older women keep busy and their lives do not appear to change as drastically although, like the men, older women do have more leisure time.

The woman opposite has everything to smile about: she typifies the older woman who still lives with family members, has strong kinship ties and enjoys good health and a comfortable standard of living. There is time to simply relax or indulge in small pleasures such as eating durians (below).

The choice of leisure activities is largely affected by the state of one's health, financial resources and whether one has the company of friends and relatives. Watching television and videos and visiting friends and relatives are the favourite activities.

More men than women enjoy reading, probably because more men of the older generation are better-educated than their female counterparts. Other leisure activities are listening to the

radio, gardening, hobbies, travel and participation in voluntary social activities.

In 1990, aged men and women made up 8 percent of the total number of participants in voluntary social activities. Most of them are in the 60–64 age group. With increasing age, participation and frequency decrease. Similarly, participation in other leisure activities also decreases, due to declining health, failing eyesight or other reasons.

While many older women enjoy working and quite a number are involved in family enterprises such as running poultry and vegetable market stalls (opposite), others prefer to broaden their horizons by watching Chinese opera (above) or learning a folk dance (below).

Mindful that Singapore is facing the prospect of a graying nation, neighbourhood community centres, clubs and other activity or social centres are paying more attention to the needs and interests of the aged. There are now more Senior Citizens' Clubs and more activities for senior citizens than ever. Between 1987 and 1991, the membership of such clubs under the People's Association alone has more than doubled, from nearly 33,000 to about 74,500. And their numbers are still growing. Numerous activities, ranging from tours and taiji to calligraphy and language classes, have been organised to cater to a wide range of interests among the members.

There is a tendency for older people to become more isolated. For those who join community activities, it is a chance to get out of the house, meet friends, keep interested in things around them and help each other out. They become more involved and their time is engaged in meaningful activity.

To further encourage the elderly to be less insular, wherever possible, activities that can accommodate both young and old may be organised to promote family togetherness. More facilities such as ramps, handrails, lifts and senior citizens' corners in void decks of housing blocks where the elderly can gather are some of the practical suggestions which would improve their quality of life further.

GROWING OLD WITH DIGNITY

People used to think that senility, illness and degeneration came inevitably with old age. Today, thanks to research, we know that senility is a medical condition and not a personality quirk of the aged, that illnesses such as diabetes and hypertension can be controlled with drugs, and the degenerative condition of the bones called osteoporosis can be prevented or stemmed with hormonal supplements and exercise.

Still, no one remains young forever and some degeneration is to be expected. The older one gets, the worse it may become, although not everyone suffers to the same extent. Most aged people can move around on their own without any help, but a good 12 percent of women over 75 need some help to move around, and about 4 percent of that age group are not able to move at all and need help most or all of the time. Strangely enough, more women than men fall into the last category. True, women live longer than men, but they are more likely than men to suffer from such chronic health conditions as osteoporosis and arthritis.

And because they outlive men, more women have to adjust to widowhood. For a woman who has always been dependent on her husband, his death can be a real threat to her financial security and can cause much anxiety. Fortunately, filial piety is still commonly practised and younger family members continue to care for their elderly emotionally and financially.

Eighty-one-year-old Mrs Loh, whose husband died more than 25 years ago, still sheds a few tears when she talks about him. She shares a flat in one of the older housing estates with her unmarried daughter.

On balance, she reckons she has a pretty good life now despite failing health. *"I can't see very well, my legs are weak and so is my heart,"* she complains, *"so I don't go out much."* Then she thinks about it and adds, *"But I'm very contented with life. I didn't expect to live so long. And my children are good to me. Half of all my children give me money – more than enough, in fact. My grandchildren visit me. … I have a good life."*

The aged population is expected to reach 20–25 percent by the year 2030 and will still increase. Although home ownership among the aged is high, in time to come, there will be more chronically sick and non-ambulant elderly men and women who would prefer to be taken care of in an institutional setting. For various reasons, they may not wish to be a burden to their family, or their family members may not be able to take care of them. Hence, there is a growing, urgent need for sheltered housing and nursing homes where these old people can be given care.

LOOK BACK, LOOK AHEAD

To young people, old age is not something they look forward to or think much about. With some planning, though, our sunset years can be close to golden.

Certain facts are in favour of the older women of today and the future. We are living in an enlightened age. We know that growing old need not mean growing decrepit and senile. Thanks to modern medicine and better nutrition, we are also stronger and healthier and have a longer life expectancy.

Women are and will continue to be better-educated, more likely to have worked outside for a significant part of their lives, have better social security upon retirement, better health and health care. They will also have a wider circle of friends and family.

They will be able to look back with content at their life achievements and look ahead to enjoying their later years, with energy to spare for community service. The older women of the future, with their education, economic independence and social and political awareness, will not be doddering grannies. They will be a force to be reckoned with.

LEGAL STATUS
Balancing the Scales

LEGAL LIGHTWEIGHTS

During the course of history, most civilisations and cultures have variously regarded women as inferior to men and have set different standards for them. Similarly, the traditions of the Chinese, Indian and Islamic cultures have held women in low regard.

The Chinese and Indians used to favour sons over daughters. A son would continue the family lineage and when he married, the family would gain a daughter-in-law. Daughters, on the other hand, would eventually marry out and become someone else's property.

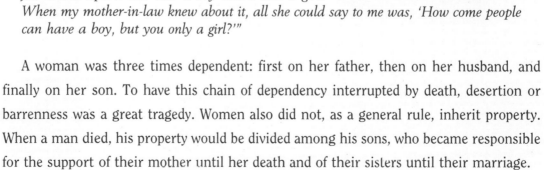

My daughter is
wild,
Helpless at her
brother.
He's hit her,
Taken her toy,
Sleeps on her bed,
While she screams
Lusts of a difficult
age.
Tears flood eyes,
Runnel down
nose,
Overrun mouth,
Moving and
morose.

—'Crybaby' by
Leong Liew Geok,
from her collec-
tion, *Love Is Not
Enough*

"When my son was born, people said to me, 'Congratulations!' but when my two daughters were born, they just smiled weakly and consoled me with 'Also good, lah,'" recalls Mrs Tay, a 60-year-old housewife. *"I got married in 1955, about the same time as my 4th brother. His wife and I had our first child just a few weeks apart. She had a boy and I had a girl. When my mother-in-law knew about it, all she could say to me was, 'How come people can have a boy, but you only a girl?'"*

A woman was three times dependent: first on her father, then on her husband, and finally on her son. To have this chain of dependency interrupted by death, desertion or barrenness was a great tragedy. Women also did not, as a general rule, inherit property. When a man died, his property would be divided among his sons, who became responsible for the support of their mother until her death and of their sisters until their marriage.

Women trapped in bad marriages could not divorce their husbands. A man, on the other hand, could divorce his wife if, for example, she were barren. Or he could simply take

another wife. Polygamy among the Chinese was allowed and having many wives was a status symbol. Hinduism allowed polygamy in certain circumstances although it was not encouraged.

In contrast, the Malay woman seems to have had tradition on her side. Malay customary law, called *adat*, was matriarchal. A husband usually moved in with the wife's family. Marriage did not change the woman's personal status. She retained control over her property and money. She was recognised as someone capable of being responsible for herself and her actions. In household arrangements, she was normally the one who held the purse strings and was the true head of the family.

Muslim law is quite different. It considers women weak, emotional and in need of the protection of men. Hence men get more than women in inheritances. A Muslim man may marry up to four wives. He can divorce his wife by pronouncing *talak* but she has to go to court and prove abuse or neglect.

English common law was introduced in Singapore in 1826 by the Second Charter of Justice and that, too, regarded women as inferior and therefore also treated them differently from men.

Under these old laws, women in Singapore, up to the 1950s, had to put up with polygamy, unequal pay (if they got to work at all) and other forms of sex discrimination. But by then there were already women, most notably the late Mrs Shirin Fozdar, who refused to put up with such discrimination any longer, and they called for equal treatment. In 1959, the People's Action Party, campaigning for seats in the Legislative Assembly, promised, among other things, 'one man, one wife', that women would be protected in their homes and that there would be equal pay for equal work.

A daughter who is 'a thousand pieces of gold' is outweighed by a son who is 'ten thousand pieces of gold'.

Mrs Shirin Fozdar (below) and other like-minded pioneers of Singapore women's rights lobbied to balance the scales.

THE REAL CHARTER OF JUSTICE

That year, the PAP won the most number of seats in the Legislative Assembly. In 1960, they introduced the Women's Charter Bill. At the second reading of the Bill, the then Minister for Labour and Law, Mr K.M. Byrne, said that it was "to consolidate the existing laws relating to marriage, divorce, the rights and duties of married persons, the maintenance of wives and children, and the punishment of offences against women and girls."

Since 1961, the Women's Charter has been updated on several occasions to keep up with changing times.

Highlights of the Women's Charter:
- *Monogamy* is the law. After 1961, the only legal marriage for everyone, except Muslims, is a monogamous one.
- *Compulsory registration* of all marriages with the Registry of Marriages. This helps to enforce monogamy.
- *Husband and wife have equal rights and duties* in running the home, in safeguarding their marriage and in caring and providing for their children.

PART VI

RIGHTS AND DUTIES OF HUSBAND AND WIFE

Rights and duties.

45.—(1) Upon the solemnization of marriage, the husband and the wife shall be mutually bound to co-operate with each other in safeguarding the interests of the union and in caring and providing for the children.

(2) The husband and the wife shall have the right separately to engage in any trade or profession or in social activities.

(3) The wife shall have the right to use her own surname and name separately.

(4) The husband and the wife shall have equal rights in the running of the matrimonial household.

CHAPTER 4 — FINANCIAL PROVISIONS CONSEQUENT ON MATRIMONIAL PROCEEDINGS

Power of court to order division of matrimonial assets

106.—(1) The court shall have power, when granting a decree of divorce, judicial separation or nullity of marriage, to order the division between the parties of any assets acquired by them during the marriage by their joint efforts or the sale of any such assets and the division between the parties of the proceeds of sale.

- *A married woman has rights*, like an unmarried woman. She is recognised as a person in her own right and can therefore sue and be sued. She can continue to use her maiden name, engage in any trade or profession, and she can acquire, hold and dispose of property in her own right.
- *A married woman can choose her domicile*. Her domicile no longer automatically follows her husband's.
- *The sole ground for divorce* is when the marriage has broken down beyond repair.
- *A married woman's property is her own*. It does not automatically become her husband's upon marriage.
- *The husband has to maintain his wife*, but she does not owe him the same duty. (This is an inequality in favour of the wife.) Both parents, though, have to maintain their children.
- *The spouse and children are protected* in cases of domestic violence.
- *Women and girls are protected* from sexual offences.

Some of the legal features of the Women's Charter require elaboration.

WHEN A MARRIAGE FAILS

A woman (or a man, for that matter) need not stay married if marriage becomes intolerable.

Under the Women's Charter, a marriage is ended by one of three ways: death, divorce or annulment.

The sole ground for a divorce is proof that the marriage has broken down beyond repair. This is indicated by any one of several situations. It may be that one partner has committed adultery and the other finds it intolerable to continue living together. One spouse may have behaved in such a way that the other cannot reasonably be expected to live with him or her; the behaviour has to be much more than petty squabbles and is usually repeated repugnant behaviour. One spouse may have deserted the other without excuse for at least two years. Husband and wife may have lived apart for three years and both consent to the divorce. Consent is not required in cases where they have lived apart for at least four years.

Divorce is not encouraged and the law does not allow a person to start divorce proceedings within three years of marriage, except in the most severe circumstances.

A marriage can also be annulled. This is where the marriage was unlawful in the first place, for instance, one of the parties is already married or is underaged, or husband and wife are too closely related. Other reasons include no proper consent and non-consummation.

In 1983, a forum on 'Career, Marriage and Parenthood' was jointly organised by SCWO (Singapore Council of Women's Organisations) and SAWL (Singapore Association of Women Lawyers). Ten years later, the questions raised then are still relevant. The challenge is far from over, but through the efforts of women of today, the future will be a much brighter one for women of tomorrow.

When the court declares the marriage ended, property owned will be divided. If the couple cannot agree to the way it is to be divided, the court will do it for them in a manner that seems fair. It will take into consideration many factors, including the needs of young children and the contribution of the partner (often the woman) who did not work, but looked after the home, the family and the children. This recognises the worth of homemaking.

Even more important than the division of matrimonial property is the rearrangement of the lives of the children. Either parent has the right to apply for custody or access to the children. The paramount consideration of the court is the welfare of the child.

MAINTENANCE OF WIFE AND CHILDREN

The Women's Charter allows a woman whose husband does not give adequate funds to maintain her to apply to the court to order him to pay her a monthly allowance or a lump sum. This right is available to Muslims as well. The court will consider the wife's financial needs and the husband's resources, so as to make a fair order.

There is no corresponding duty for a woman to maintain a needy husband. This is probably because the Women's Charter was enacted at a time when the norm was for a man to be the principal breadwinner while the wife was the homemaker. She was economically

inactive and needed the protection of the law.

Both parents, however, must provide for the children as the Charter recognises that parental care should be shared equally by both parents. Legitimate and illegitimate children, and even other people's children who have been accepted as part of the family, such as stepchildren, can claim for maintenance.

A divorced woman can claim for reasonable maintenance from her ex-husband as well. Theoretically, this right continues until she dies or remarries, but the court will only order what seems fair to both parties.

DOMESTIC VIOLENCE

Even in the best of homes, domestic violence may erupt. If it is not serious, the police will treat it as domestic 'misunderstanding' and advise the couple to sort out their differences themselves in an amicable manner. But sadly, there are times when the violence gets out of hand and intervention is necessary.

'Violence' is not defined in the Women's Charter. The courts have confined the meaning to attacks of physical violence or threats of such violence. A spouse who has suffered such forms of violence can apply to the courts for a personal protection order whereby the violent spouse is directed to refrain from violence. It is also possible to apply for a domestic exclusion order which requires the violent spouse to refrain from coming home during the period that the order is in force.

SEXUAL CRIMES AGAINST WOMEN

The Women's Charter also seeks to protect women and girls against sexual crimes. It therefore makes, among other things, prostitution, trafficking of women and girls for prostitution, and sexual intercourse with a girl under 16 (except if lawfully married to her), punishable offences.

Other sexual offences such as rape, incest, outrage of modesty and the use of criminal force against women are punishable by the Penal Code. Rape is a very serious crime and is

Violence against women is unfortunately a reality which Asian women tend to keep quiet about. Organisations such as AWARE (Association of Women for Action and Research) remind us by way of exhibitions, books and talks that women have a right not to be violated.

punishable with up to 20 years in prison, a fine and caning. Incest is also a serious offence. If the victim is under 14 years of age, a man could face up to 14 years in prison. (A woman could also be convicted of incest although the maximum prison sentence for her is 5 years.)

Outraging of modesty, depending on the circumstances, has a maximum sentence of 10 years in prison and caning. Men who use criminal force on a woman, such as intentionally pushing himself against her without her consent, knowing it would frighten or annoy her, can expect a maximum prison sentence of three months, or a fine, or both. 'Sexual harassment' is not a crime in our statutes, although if any physical force is used, it will be punishable.

MUSLIM LAW

Muslims in Singapore marry and divorce by Muslim law, which is administered by the Syariah Court. The Syariah Court hears matters regarding marriage, divorce, division of property, maintenance, and other things pertaining to Muslim law.

Singapore Muslim women today have much the same rights as non-Muslim women, but

certain differences remain. A Muslim man is allowed to marry up to four wives and he can divorce his wife by pronouncing *talak*. In practice, however, these rights cannot be exercised on a whim. He has to go before a *kathi*, an official of the Syariah Court, before he can marry a second time and his *talak* must be registered to be effective. The *kathi* will also counsel a couple seeking a divorce. The involvement of the *kathi* ensures that Muslim men do not abuse their privileges.

"THE BEST THING ..."

It is possible to have a baby and a career at the same time (opposite). Women are entitled to, among other things, paid maternity leave.

The Women's Charter is not a real charter as it does not cover the rights of women exhaustively. But it is central to the status of Singapore women and is a progressive piece of legislation. In the 1970s, Singapore women were the envy of other Asian women. Mrs Azah Aziz, a prominent Malaysian journalist who was interviewed in the 1980 *Her World Annual,* said, "The best thing that happened to Singapore [women] in the 1960s was the Women's Charter."

The Women's Charter marked the start of women's rights in Singapore and also set the direction for other legislation towards the equal treatment of women and men. While we do not have a specific anti-discrimination law, what matters is that, in everyday life, anything men may legally do, so may women – vote, study, work ...

But biological differences are undeniable – women can have babies; men cannot. So the Employment Act provides for maternity benefits and restricts working hours for pregnant women.

If a woman has served her employer for at least six months before she gives birth, she is entitled to two months' paid maternity leave for her first two children. Her employer may not terminate her service within three months of her giving birth without good reason, nor during her maternity leave. Pregnant women, too, are protected in that they cannot be made to work at night without their consent and a doctor's letter certifying them fit.

WHAT MORE?

In recent years, some suggestions have been put forward by women's groups and others to further protect women and their families.

Be it in education, work or other areas, women do not have to be satisfied with lesser options than their male counterparts.

CPF contributions form part of an employee's retirement benefits and they are alike for men and women employees, but one particular group of workers has been forgotten – the homemakers. Their work is valuable work that does not bring monetary rewards. Women's groups have been calling for change in this area, perhaps by putting aside part of the husband's CPF funds for the wife while he is still working, so that these women are also provided for in their old age.

Some lawyers feel that a Family Court should be established where all proceedings and matters related to the family can be heard under one roof.

At present, divorces are heard in the High Court, adoptions may be heard in either the High Court or the Subordinate Courts and applications for maintenance are filed in the Subordinate Courts. An average layperson seeking aid from the courts will find herself in a legal maze. A Family Court, where there would also be counsellors and social workers on hand to assist the Court and the family, will surely be a boon to a family in distress.

By and large, our laws are non-discriminatory. It might therefore surprise quite a few people to know that nowhere is it written in our Constitution that women are not to be discriminated against. Not that they really mind. Most women feel that the substance is more important than the form.

Yes, in substance Singapore women have equality and they are definitely better off now than they have ever been. But there remain some areas of unequal treatment which are incongruous with women's desire to be viewed

completely as equal and complementary partners of men.

One example are the citizenship laws. A child who is born in Singapore to at least one Singaporean parent will be a Singaporean by birth. However, if the child is born outside Singapore, the Constitution states that the father must be Singaporean in order for the child to qualify to be a Singaporean by descent. The child does not qualify if only the *mother* is Singaporean.

Another is the practice that gives medical benefits to the wife and children of a male civil servant, but not the husband and children of a female civil servant, except where she is divorced, widowed, or when her husband can no longer work because of serious illness. This was probably carried over from the old days when the men were the sole breadwinners. Those days are long gone. Perhaps it is time the scheme be changed to reflect this reality.

Women, young and old, now know their rights and how to assert them. But the struggle will never see an end if men and boys are not similarly educated to shed their cultural prejudices as well.

Overleaf: Girls from junior colleges in fatigues for an army 'familiarisation' exercise. Women who want to serve in Singapore's defence forces can do so.

So where do we go from here? Some have said women in Singapore have it much better than women in most other Asian countries and even in some countries in the West. They point out also that men have to do National Service while women do not, so we should not clamour for more. Others may feel that 'so-far-so-good' is 'not-good-enough', that we should never stop striving for the ideal.

We have come so far, can we not go further?

WOMEN IN THE PUBLIC EYE
Road to the Top

WOMEN GLADIATORS

Women constitute 50 percent of the population. They form 40 percent of the workforce. What role do they play in the political life of the country?

Between 1970 when the late Mdm Chan Choy Siong retired from politics and 1984 when three woman MPs were elected to parliament, there was a 14-year hiatus in women's representation in the highest law-making body of the country. Today, we have two elected and one nominated woman MPs. This is only 3 percent, much lower than the world average of 5–10 percent, which is already low enough.

Of course, women's participation in public life involves not just parliamentary representation. It includes also women's representation at the executive committee level in the trade unions, civic associations, grassroots organisations and so on. The figures are not fantastic.

Why is this so?

Before World War II, women in Singapore did not play any role in politics at all. Neither did the men, because the colonial system did not allow anyone to participate in public

The schoolgirl activist (below) at a demonstration in 1961 and the young woman of the nineties (opposite) can both aspire to great heights, although the woman of the nineties is more likely to favour the intellectual as opposed to the militant approach.

affairs except in a very nominal way. And then, women were just beginning to receive an education in schools established by missions and local associations.

In 1948, women in Singapore got the right to vote. Unlike women in the West, we did not have to fight for that right. It was handed to us by the British colonial administration. It was not until the second half of the 1950s that women's organisations began to press for reforms in women's status. Pioneers like Mrs Shirin Fozdar

and Mrs George Lee were gaining support from women in speaking out against sex discrimination and other injustices. The need for change was palpable. Soon, women's reformist efforts were caught up with the fervent movement to gain independence for Singapore, and many English- and Chinese-educated women began to participate in local politics. Political awareness was high, and women were drawn into the anti-colonial and anti-communist struggles of this turbulent period in our history.

In 1959, the year Singapore gained self-government, women's rights was one of the issues during the elections to the Legislative Assembly. That year, as many as nine women ran for election, and five went in. Mdm Chan Choy Siong was among the four PAP women candidates elected, while Mrs Seow Peck Leng was from an opposition party. In 1961, to cap the efforts of all women activists, the Women's Charter was passed.

Women continued to participate actively in the 1963 election, with eleven candidates running. Only two from the PAP and one from the Barisan Socialis were returned.

After Singapore became an independent nation on 9 August 1965, national security, economic development and other immediate concerns were uppermost in people's minds and gained the government's urgent attention. It was certainly not a time to mull over

Political awareness was at an all-time high in 1959. Four of the five PAP women seen here on the steps of City Hall were elected to the Legislative Assembly. Left to right: Oh Shu Chen, Fung Yin Ching (partly hidden), Chan Choy Siong, Sahorah bte Ahmat and Ho Puay Choo.

In the 1980s, the press carried arguments in favour of greater participation of women in politics. Those who dared question women's fitness to enter politics were given short shrift in editorials and letters to the press (here and overleaf).

women's issues. In 1968, only Mdm Chan Choy Siong was elected to Parliament, being uncontested. And when she retired from politics in 1970, Parliament was left without any female MP for the next 14 years.

But the path had already been paved for women to progress and, indeed, they did. Women became better-educated, more went out to work, they got better jobs and their economic status improved. They had become an important component of the nation's economic growth. Women then found that while their importance and responsibilities had increased, they were not getting the sort of support they needed to enable them to discharge their responsibilities.

Holding a full-time job, managing the home and bringing up the children all at the same time is a trying experience by any standard. Sometimes it is virtually impossible to shoulder the burden. To help them cope, women have been asking for more and better childcare facilities, options for part-time work, flexible working hours and no-pay leave, without having to compromise seniority, advancement and training prospects.

In the mid-1980s, there were other social issues of particular concern to women. The various population policies was one. First it was 'Two Is Enough', then, because of a declining birthrate, it was 'Have Three Or More If You Can Afford It'. Then, of course, there was the Great Marriage Debate that raged on for quite a while. Like it or not, women found their biological and social roles, which are essentially very private and sensitive matters, the subject of widespread national discussion.

A new generation of educated women began to speak their minds. Because their demands were seen as both sensible and reasonable, the public began to pay more attention to them. The fact that women and 'women's issues' have an important role to play in nation building is undeniable. Half the population is women and their growing presence in the workforce means that 'women's issues' are not just women's problems; they are national issues. Women and their views need to be represented and incorporated into the decision-making process.

Women MPs of 1988–1991 (opposite), from left to right, Dr Seet Ai Mee, Mrs Yu-Foo Yee Shoon, Dr Aline Wong and Dr Dixie Tan.

Chan Heng Chee (right), a political scientist voted Singapore's first Woman of the Year in 1992, was once ambassador to the United Nations. She is now director of the Singapore International Foundation and the Institute of Southeast Asian Studies.

In the general elections of 1984, a total of six women stood for elections. Three were from opposition parties and three from the PAP. Only those from the PAP were successful: Dr Dixie Tan, a medical doctor; Dr Aline Wong, a university lecturer; and Mrs Yu-Foo Yee Shoon, a trade unionist. These three women, educated and articulate, had already been much involved in social and community work related to women, the family and the underprivileged. They were the new women in politics.

Although all three women emphasised that they should be viewed as MPs and not just female MPs, they boosted women's morale and were seen as a fillip for women's rights in Singapore. They did so through raising women's issues in Parliament. That they were highly visible in the public eye made them role models for other women and it was inevitable that there were great expectations of them to champion women's causes.

The nature of women's causes has changed with the times. In the 1960s and 1970s, the problem was fighting inbred prejudices and blatant discrimination. By the 1980s, the cause had become a lot subtler, but in no way diminished. Dr Wong's views reflect this change. In her report, *Economic Development and Women's Place: Women in Singapore*, published in 1980, she acknowledges the overall improvement of the Singapore woman's status, then she points out that the "question is not simply whether inequality between the sexes still exists" but whether the interests of women are incorporated in state planning. In other words, integration.

In an interview in 1991, she reiterates her conviction that "women's issues are not separate from

societal issues," and the way to tackle them is not to overemphasise the separateness of women, but to view them in the broader perspective of social and economic development issues.

Dr Wong is representative of these new women in politics who realise that lasting solutions to women's problems cannot be found in ad hoc remedies. They have to be tackled at the very roots that lie in society's structure, attitudes, customs and culture.

Four years later, in 1988, they were joined by a fourth woman MP, Dr Seet Ai Mee, a clinical biochemist. Like them, she was articulate, knowledgeable and very much involved in social and community work. Shortly after the elections, Dr Seet made history for women in Singapore when she was appointed Minister of State for Education and Community Development, and later promoted to Acting Minister for Community Development. More crushing, then, was her narrow defeat in the 1991 general elections. With Dr Dixie Tan's retirement from politics, the total number of women in Parliament went down to two. In September 1992, Dr Kanwaljit Soin, an orthopaedic surgeon, became a Nominated MP.

From Day One as Nominated MP, Dr Soin, founding member and current President of AWARE (Association of Women for Action and Research) made it her mission to speak on women's behalf in national policy-making. But, like Dr Wong, she believes that there are no 'separate' women's issues. "Violence against a woman is an ethical issue, a working woman is an economic issue and childcare is a family issue. Every issue that involves a woman involves one aspect of society."

On 2 July 1989, the PAP Women's Wing was launched (right), yet another step forward for women in politics.

Left: Dr Aline Wong, Minister of State for Health, Chairman of the PAP Women's Wing, sociologist turned politician.

Women's re-entry into Parliament rekindled an interest in both the ruling and opposition parties to field more women candidates in the 1988 and 1991 elections. Are we witnessing a resurgence of women's issues in response to women's changing needs and aspirations? Or are we simply recognising women's influence as voters? In 1989, the PAP set up its Women's Wing. Chaired by Dr Aline Wong, its aim is to raise political awareness of women and to encourage more of them to enter politics. Will women, being doubly loaded with work and family, be able and willing to come forward and take on a third responsibility?

WOMEN UNITED

The industrialisation of the 1960s and 1970s drew women to the workforce like iron filings to a magnet. Likewise, the proportion of women members in trade unions swelled from only 17 percent in 1964 to 44 percent in 1991.

In 1973, the NTUC Women's Committee was formed. In the mid-1970s, unions were encouraged to set up their own women's committees. In order to better coordinate their activities, the Women's Programme Secretariat was set up in 1976 with the main objectives of helping the women members become better persons and workers, and to help provide support services. Its first full-time Secretary was Mrs Yu-Foo Yee Shoon, who served from 1976 to 1982. In 1980, Mrs Yu-Foo set another precedent for women in the unions when she was made Chairman of the NTUC, the highest office ever achieved by any woman in the trade union movement.

Over the years, with the nature of women's jobs evolving, the Women's Secretariat has included leadership training as well, although its primary objective remains the enhancement of the women workers' welfare.

Activities were concentrated on social, recreational and educational areas to draw more women into the labour movement. The Secretariat also looked into the perennial problem of working women who stopped work after marriage and childbirth because of the lack of good and affordable childcare services. The NTUC took over the management of ten childcare centres from the then Social Welfare Department. Under the leadership of Mrs Yu-Foo, they expanded and improved on the quality of the services. Today, the NTUC is the single largest provider of childcare facilities, catering to around 2,000 children. The NTUC has also repeatedly urged the government to implement measures – such as part-time and flexitime work – that would attract more women to work.

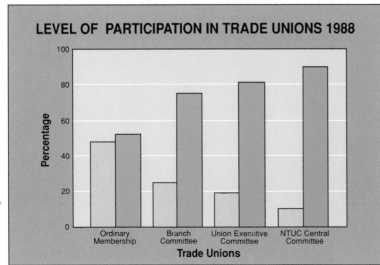

Nonetheless, women are still struggling with demands at home and at work. Few have the luxury of entertaining thoughts of leadership. This is reflected by the fact that women make up 42 percent of total union membership, but they are a mere sprinkling as union leaders. Moreover, the proportion of women in leadership positions decreases with each higher level of leadership.

The main reasons are nothing new. Only full-time workers can join unions. Of these, most of the women already have their plates full being workers, wives and mothers. That leaves them precious little time for anything else.

Besides, tradition runs deep and many men are still not ready for powerful women. Nor are some women comfortable with competing for and being in positions of leadership and power. Women have achieved much in the

Although women are a minority in the NTUC central committee (below), its Assistant Secretary-General is a woman, Mrs Yu-Foo Yee Shoon (above), seen here at one of the many childcare centres run by the NTUC.

LEVEL OF PARTICIPATION IN TRADE UNIONS 1988

Percentage / Trade Unions

Female / Male

Ordinary Membership · Branch Committee · Union Executive Committee · NTUC Central Committee

Personal satisfaction can be achieved in a number of ways. Betty Chen (right), seen here with a participant of the Henderson Senior Citizens' Home of which she is the Chairman, finds fulfilment in charity work.

home and work arenas, but they still fight shy of public life.

This is not an insurmountable problem. Things have changed and they will no doubt continue to change. In time to come, when gender stereotypes cease to be the norm and as women get used to speaking their minds and exercising their intellects, there will be more women who will aspire towards and attain public office.

Helping to create greater awareness of women's issues for and among women is the Singapore Council of Women's Organisations (SCWO). Formed in 1980 with only 15 affiliates, in 1992 it had 36 affiliates, with 94 thousand members that include housewives, factory workers, business women and professionals.

One of the SCWO's main objectives is "to promote and improve the status of women in general, and particularly, in education, economics, social welfare and community involvement, culture and sports." To do this, it provides a resource centre and a forum for women's groups, and disseminates information in a monthly newsletter on issues that range from health to challenges of working women and international affairs concerning women.

Flair and a fine eye for detail earned Chua Gek Noi (opposite) the top award in the Hong Kong Diamond Design competition barely six years after she entered the field of jewellery design.

Right: Mrs Jaya Mohideen, Singapore's former Ambassador to Belgium.

MAKING THEIR MARK

A young woman looking for a job in the 1920s would have teaching and nursing as the only respectable options open to her. Nowadays, ask any modern little girl what her ambition is, and her answer will probably not be very different from that of a little boy's. Doctor, astronaut, lawyer, engineer, movie star, whatever.

Somewhere at the start of this amazing metamorphosis in the mid-1950s, women practically swamped the production lines, with about 83 percent of all working women employed on them. Of the rest, less than 10 percent held professional and technical jobs, about 6.5 percent were in clerical, sales and service-oriented jobs and a miserly 0.4 percent were administrators and managers.

As more and more women became educated, they learnt very quickly that the new system rewards talent and diligence. By 1990, the percentage of women on production lines fell by half while administrators and managers increased tenfold.

During those years when our economy was expanding rapidly, new jobs and positions were created and women were recruited along with the men. Then those who were good discovered that there was room at the top. Today, there are many women holding senior

positions in banks and securities companies. One of the most notable is Mrs Elizabeth Sam, Executive Vice-President of OCBC and former Chairman of SIMEX. Other women bankers have said that, by her ability and professionalism, she paved the way for other women to enter the sombre, male-dominated world of banking.

The other fields in which women have progressed are retailing, advertising and publishing. Women in these fields used to be just the support base to the senior staff who were usually men. These days, you will find quite a number of women at board meetings and they are not there to take the minutes either. Some others have decided to strike out on their own.

Those who say women do not have a head for figures are lost for words when they meet Elizabeth Sam of the OCBC (left).

Rachel Swee (right), is an accountant turned entrepreneur, while Jannie Tay (below right) started out as a shopgirl and is now the managing director of a chain of luxury stores.

The climb up the corporate ladder is never easy for anyone, but a woman is often handicapped by sexual stereotypes, prejudices, young children clamouring for attention and the constant tussle between home and career. They are riddled by guilt feelings and, more often than not, they bear the brunt when things go wrong at home. It is a fact that while many modern husbands may be proud of their wives making good, they still expect them to play the role of 'the little woman' in social settings. All this merely serves to complicate and confuse the roles expected of women.

But women are not to be deterred. They know that perseverance is a vital ingredient for success and they are not afraid of hard work. Nor sacrifice, for that matter, if that proves necessary. Mrs Doreen Phua, wife, mother and woman with a vision, went into scientific publishing in 1980 and is now the managing director of a fast-growing company. She was

one of the first women entrepreneurs granted pioneer industry status by the EDB.

Another entrepreneur and pioneer is Rachel Swee. An accountant with no formal training in computers, she ventured into the high-tech computer software industry and made a success of it. In fact, she became the winner of Singapore's first award of Small Businessman of the Year.

Q: What does it take for a woman entrepreneur to be a success?

A: Whatever it takes a man entrepreneur – and a bit more.

"We are afraid to take risks and are too careful. A woman entrepreneur must learn to take calculated risks. Similarly, we must learn to take failures. We tend to be too sensitive to setbacks and are prone to excessive worrying."

"As women, we have our strengths and weaknesses and it is important to identify them. For example, we should not try to be like a man. We can be assertive without being aggressive."

"We should also turn our weaknesses to strengths, such as sensitivity, compassion and patience."

—Su Yeang, a graphic and industrial designer who set up her own design company in 1983, in an interview with *Singapore Professionals* in 1989.

In the glamorous, glitzy fashion industry is Esther Tay, Singapore's first fashion designer to break into the tight Japanese market.

In the world of expensive jewellery and time-pieces is Mrs Jannie Tay, well-known on the local social scene, who is managing director of a listed company with a chain of upmarket outlets selling luxury watches.

There are yet others who turned their passions into businesses. Regina Wong has always loved precious stones. She also knows a good business opportunity when she sees one and turned her love of gems and jewels into a lucrative business. In 1972, she started her own jewellery company, which has grown into one of Singapore's better-known jewellers.

Art can be a very poor paymaster. Witness the number of late, great painters, musicians and writers who died as paupers. But all is not lost. There are artists who have made something out of their art. Many women have used their talents and made significant achievements.

Som Said, choreographer, dancer, make-up artiste, costume designer and artistic director, turned her prodigious talent and passion into a successful business. She received the Ministry of Community Development's Cultural Medallion in 1987 for her contribution to Malay dance. Her bridal shop exploits her creativity in costume design and make-up.

Som Said (above) takes time off her business to help children in the voluntary group Sriwana develop grace and discipline through dance performances.

Opposite: Esther Tay, breaking into the Japanese apparel market.

110

People who love what they do cannot help infecting others with their enthusiasm. Aziza Ali is seen opposite with her restaurant staff.

Right and overleaf: Goh Soo Khim, artistic director of Singapore Dance Theatre, has a gift for inspiring and nurturing young and talented dancers.

Another dancer who has combined artistic talent and good management with success is Goh Soo Khim, who established the thriving Singapore Dance Theatre. A highly respected figure in the regional dance scene, she has been closely associated with the growth of ballet in Singapore, especially since she became Director and Principal of the Singapore Ballet Academy in 1971.

It takes brilliance to turn a love for food into gold. It took Aziza Ali to elevate Malay food to cuisine level in her restaurant which bears her mark everywhere – from the food to the decor and down to the cutlery. Her road to success was not easy. Her parents had objected to her plans initially as they felt that it was unbecoming for a Malay girl to venture into business. But she persisted.

These women are but a handful of the many success stories that resound throughout Singapore. Each is a story of hard work and determination, of finding a satisfactory balance between work and a personal life. Ultimately, it is a story of true grit and a steadfast conviction when things did not go well.

They have shown the next generation of women that ambition is not a dirty word, that being feminine is not anathema to success, that there is no need to feel guilty for wanting to make something of our lives. We are no lesser than men, and this system of meritocracy allows us to reach our full potential as human beings.

The stars, it seems, are finally within our grasp.

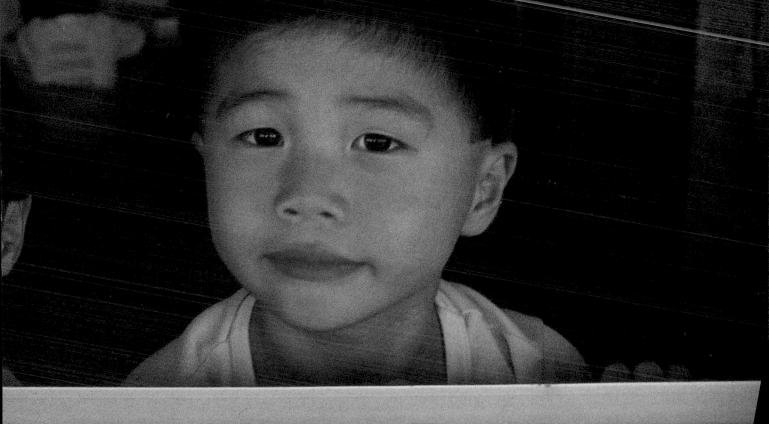

ACKNOWLEDGEMENTS

The PAP Women's Wing Executive Committee gratefully acknowledges
the following foundations, corporations, individuals and groups whose
generous sponsorship helped make this book possible:

Lee Foundation
The Shaw Foundation

Diamond Industries Pte Ltd
Global Airfreight International Pte Ltd
Hitachi Zosen Singapore (Pte) Ltd
Jing Quee Chin Joo & Teck Hui
JeTaime Jewellers Pte Ltd
Jurong Shipyard Ltd
Komoco Auto Pte Ltd
Lim Manufacturing Pte Ltd
Prima Ltd
Singapore Shipbuilding & Engineering Ltd
Times Editions Pte Ltd

Ang Beng Choo
Ang Hung Hwa
Akiko Aw
Ellen Aw Yeong Sow Ngan
Dorothy Chan
Betty Chen
E.S. Chew
Melanie Chew
Anne Choo Chok Ann
Kathleen M. Chopard
Chua Li Eng
Diana Eu
Fang Ai Lian
Theresa Foo-Yo Mie Yoen
Geh Min
Alice Goh
Goh Bee Eng
Laura Hwang

Eddie Lee-Ong Siew Kuan
Ellen Lee
Lee Chin Neo
Jenny Lim
Margaret Loh
Annie Loke
Shirley Loo-Lim
Low Sin Leng
Gretchen Liu
J. Mohideen
Angela Ng Beng Hua
Dorothy Ng
Tisa Ng
May B.Y. Oh
Ong Siew Eng
Ong Siew May
Ong Yam Chua
Pauline Ong-Tsang

Ow Hong Kee
Doreen Phua
Quek-Chua Bin Hwee
Vemala Rajamanickam
Elizabeth Sam
Seow Peck Leng
Soh Tuan Heng
Kanwaljit Soin
Su Yeang
Tan Soo Khoon
Anamah Tan
Dixie Tan
Lilian Tan
Marilyn Tan
Nancy Tey
Wee Eng Hwa
Annie Wee
Ann Yeoh-Chan

PAP Changkat Branch
PAP Yuhua Branch

PHOTO CREDITS

APA Photo Agency S'pore 6, 19 (top),
   45 (bottom), 62 (centre), 92
AWARE 87
Marcus Brooke/Pro-file 69
Rex Butcher/Pro-file 25
Wendy Chan/Image Bank S'pore 80 (top),
   85, 96
Colin Cheong 120
Jean Léo Dugast/APA 59, 63
Alain Evrard/APA 53
Family Planning Unit 22 (top, bottom left
   & right), 23 (top)
Foo Check Woo 80 (bottom)
Gerald Gay 76-77
Rio Helmi 109 (top & bottom)
Ho Khee Tong 18 (bottom)
Hans Hoefer/APA 61 (bottom)
Housing & Development Board 65 (bottom)
Indeco 73

Ivan Ho 19 (bottom)
Ingo Jezierski 2-3
Ingo Jezierski/APA 48 (top)
Mark Law 16, 17, 33, 38, 47, 50, 55, 58, 60,
   70 (top & bottom), 72 (top), 74, 78, 79, 88,
   102, 105, 106, 108, 111, 112, 113, 114-115,
   118
Alan Lee, Her World 100
Leong Ka Tai 18 (top)
Albert Lim 29
Lawrence Lim 14-15, 30-31, 34-35, 36 (top &
   bottom), 43 (top), 45 (top), 67, 104, 110
Philip Little/APA 28, 71 (top)
Susan Loh 37 (top)
Patrick Lucero/APA 51
Joe Lynch/APA 32 (top)
Peter Mealin 54, 116-117
Ministry of Information and the Arts
   32 (bottom), 39 (bottom), 52, 61 (top),
   65 (top), 72 (bottom left), 81, 83, 98

Nicky Moey 39 (top)
Nanyang Girls' High School 40 (top)
New Paper 94-95
Robin Nichols/APA 93
People's Association 71 (bottom),
   72 (bottom right)
Dominic Sansoni/Pro-file 23 (bottom),
   49, 66, 68
Singapore Chinese Girls' School 40 (bottom),
   41 (top & bottom)
Singapore International Foundation 57, 107
Singapore Polytechnic 43 (bottom), 44,
   46, 75 (top), 90, 91
Social Development Unit 20 (top & bottom),
   21
Straits Times 24, 37 (bottom), 48 (bottom),
   62 (top & bottom), 75 (bottom), 84, 97
Tuck Loong 4, 8, 10, 12
Russell Wong 101

"My marriage wasn't wonderful, but I never thought of blaming anyone because I married a man of my own choosing, unlike some of my friends who were matchmade. I always say, you want rights, then you also have responsibility."

"We must involve women in the decision-making process. We must take into account women's interests whenever we make policy decisions that affect women in particular."

"Women's issues are not separate from societal issues ...The thing that comes out clearly is that women's issues should be integrated with development issues and other processes that change society. Women's issues must be viewed within these broader development issues."

"No such thing [divorce] at the time. Father, mother also won't allow you to come back. Those times, not supposed to go back to parents' house. You just stick it out."

"... it is too often forgotten that many women, who have internalised society's conservative attitudes towards their sex, have eventually scaled down their own aspiration and simply reconciled themselves to their traditionally defined roles."

"I definitely want babies. As many as I can have. Well, maybe three. It's not important, but it's nice to have the children of the man you love. It's probably the example set by my mother. She devoted her life to bringing up my sister and me and only went back to work when I was 12."

"Female revolutionaries are rare flowers and they do not tend to keep their bloom for very long. Unless, of course, as has happened in Singapore, the revolution is a quiet one ..."